ISBN 978-1-334-36156-2
PIBN 10022744

1 MONTH OF
FREE
READING

at

www.ForgottenBooks.com

By purchasing this book you are eligible for one month membership to ForgottenBooks.com, giving you unlimited access to our entire collection of over 1,000,000 titles via our web site and mobile apps.

To claim your free month visit:

www.forgottenbooks.com/free22744

MASTERS OF RUSSIAN MUSIC

GLINKA

BY

M. MONTAGU-NATHAN
AUTHOR OF "A HISTORY OF RUSSIAN MUSIC"

NEW YORK
DUFFIELD AND COMPANY
1917

CONTENTS

GLINKA

INTRODUCTION

THE life-work of Glinka is the outcome of a yearning to endow his fatherland with a musical treasury that it could really call its own. But he was inspired rather by the instinct that this could be done than by a recognition of the need for its accomplishment.

The pioneers who followed him, such as Dargomijsky, Balakiref, Cui, Moussorgsky, and Rimsky-Korsakof, were reformers. They were intolerant of past methods, and especially of past abuses, and set up for themselves an ideal for the future which should shame the past. Their propaganda concerned what they felt ought to be the condition of music in Russia, and they strove with all their might to bring about this desired condition. Glinka was not—in the active sense of the term—a reformer. He sought the right, but did not concern himself much about the wrong. His inauguration of Russian musical nationalism did not arise from an exasperation provoked by a survey of the past, but from a desire that the future should bring with it something of which to be proud. He was simply an initiator.

Instinct was the first cause behind every significant step that he took. The impulse to create a music that should make his countrymen feel "really at home" was instinctive. Behind his resolve to visit Spain— in order to seek out a folk-music that in its link with the Orient has a quality in common with that of Russia—was instinct. The belief that Russian folk-songs might have their origin in the ancient ecclesiastical music was not founded upon erudition, but was intuitive.

Glinka was not of the stuff of which reformers are made. All his life an impaired constitution made him something between a valetudinarian and a hypo-chondriac. The pages of his Memoirs form quite a catalogue of drugs—a long-roll of physicians. His dread of illness was equalled only by his terror of death. Despite these physical and mental conditions, he accomplished something of which a very giant of health might have been proud.

He vitalized the folk-tunes not merely of one but of two nations. His legacy to Russian music has been shared by the world.

The condition of music in Russia when Glinka appeared on the scene was not such as might be expected inevitably to have inspired the great achievement that now stands to the composer's credit. Of music there was plenty to be heard. And even to one who looked upon music as "my soul," there might not have seemed any call for the devotion of a life to an attempt to add to the existing number of masterpieces. Again, considering that the music heard in Russia was at that time for the most part

European, such a man as Glinka might well have been satisfied that the work of his precursors Fomin, Alabief, Cavos, and Verstovsky, constituted a sufficient step in the direction of emancipation. To him they might easily have appeared in sufficient contrast to the music coming from a Western source to be considered adequately national in character. One presumes that their composers themselves thought so.

Since the time of Peter the Great the foreigner had been sure of a welcome in Russia. In literary and musical life the foreign product, for a long time after Peter's "window into Europe" had been opened, was alone deemed worthy of notice. The immense store of folk-song that has been collected during the last sixty years had previously been more or less under a ban, owing to the refusal of the Church to sanction the references it contained to pagan deities and ceremonials. And the native musician was a humble being, on whose part any attempt to proclaim the existence of Russian music would in all probability have been regarded as an abominable heresy.

The middle of the eighteenth century had seen an Italian musician established in the patronage of the Crown. The Empress Anne's invitation to Francesco Araya was the beginning of a long era of Italian domination. Elizabeth, her successor, appears to have entertained a belief that France might be worthy of an art that could at least be allowed comparison with that of Italy. But Catherine the Great, despite her partiality for French philosophy, pinned her faith to the music of the more southerly land, and quite an array of distinguished Italians received the Imperial invitation during her reign.

To her, however, must be given the credit of having attempted to improve the condition of native music. Elizabeth had gone so far as to encourage the use of the language in operatic librettos. Catherine went the length of writing a libretto on a Russian subject, and this example was of course followed by composers of humbler rank.

Had the tradition introduced by Catherine continued to flourish, the sudden awakening that took place toward the middle of the nineteenth century might never have occurred; it would not have been needed. But for reasons of state, no doubt, Alexander I. saw fit to reinstate French music in the favour of the Court. The presiding genius was Boieldieu. The home product began once more to occupy an entirely subordinate position, and the nourishment given it by its Imperial foster-mother was thrown away.

But with the events of 1812, a dormant Russian patriotism suddenly raised its head. Rostopschin's flames caused another fire to be kindled. The Russian nation awoke to the consciousness that it was good to be Russian. A national feeling was aroused that has never since subsided.

At the time of the Moscow conflagration, Glinka was eight years old. By the time that he left Russia on the visit to Italy, the national sentiment had grown sufficiently strong to act as a stimulant to the musical patriotism prompted by what in his Memoirs he describes as nostalgia.

The auspicious moment had arrived, and fortunately, with the moment, the man. The "*patriotisme feroce de Rostopschine*," while preparing the mind of Glinka, had affected also the spirit of the public. Hence the success of "A Life for the Tsar."

The influence of "Russlan and Ludmilla" was more subtle and much less speedily felt. In the late 'fifties it was commonly voted tedious by the average music-lover in Petrograd. It had captured the esteem of a few progressive musicians, but even as late as in 1870 it was thought necessary by the Opera Directorate to make huge "cuts" in the score.

Among musicians it had by this time, however, really begun to make itself felt. In Rimsky-Korsakof's Memoirs may be read the account of its influence upon the young Lyadof, whose enthusiasm for the work found vent in solitary renderings, before his bedroom mirror, of the principal rôles in the opera. But it is in the symphonic and operatic output of the writer of those "Chronicles of My Musical Life," and in the works of his associates, Balakiref, Borodin, and Moussorgsky, that lies the best possible testimony to the extraordinary influence of Glinka's second opera upon the immediately succeeding generation.

And even to-day, when Russian musicians have begun to protest against the assumption that they are bound by tradition to the national subject, there is among the greatest and most progressive one whose music proclaims him to be of the faithful. The music of Kashchei's approach in " The Fire-Bird," and that of the Chinese Emperor in " The Nightingale," is instinct with the spirit of Chernomor's March in " Russlan and Ludmilla."

The tradition founded by Glinka is not then simply a tradition ordaining the use of folk-tunes and native subjects in Russian music. It is that of putting the very Soul of Russia into her music. If Glinka did not himself achieve as much as this, it is he who showed the way.

PART I

CAREER

I.

"I was born," wrote Michael Ivanovich Glinka, in his Memoirs, "at dawn on 20th May, 1804, in the village of Novospasskoi, the property of my father, Ivan Nikolayevich Glinka, who was a retired army captain." Having described the rustic surroundings of his birthplace, he continues: "Soon after my birth my mother, Evgenia Andreyevna, *née* Glinka, was obliged to confide my upbringing to my maternal grandmother, Thyokla Aleksandrovna, who, having taken possession of me, removed me to her room where, together with my two nurses, I spent the next three or four years, seldom seeing my parents. As a child, I was delicate, and subject to nervous and other disorders; my grandmother, an aged lady, was almost always unwell, and her room, in which I was confined, was kept at a temperature never lower than 20 degrees Réaumur."

His grandmother indulged him in every possible way, and but for his naturally amiable disposition would have wrought as great havoc with his character as she did with his constitution. The signature

" Mimosa," to be found beneath some of the letters
in his published correspondence, bears witness to the
fact that he was fully aware of the source of the physical
troubles with which throughout his life he was beset.
His grandmother had made of him a sensitive plant.

It is not to be wondered at that, with such an
upbringing, the child should have become quite unlike
the average youngster of his age; his first efforts to
amuse himself were such as are rarely to be observed
in a nursery. He was "piously inclined," drew
pictures of churches in chalk on the floor, and appro-
priately followed this up, as soon as he could read—
which was at a remarkably early age—by reciting
passages from the Scriptures so impressively as to
bring tears to the eyes of his doting grandmother and
her elderly cronies.

His musical predispositions were manifested by a
craving for every kind of bell-sounds; he sought to
imitate the clanging that penetrated the walls of the
house by playing bell-ringer on two copper vessels.
When he was unwell he was given some small hand-
bells that appear to have served to maintain a strength
of spirit. Presently his fondness for the Bible gave
place to a keen interest in books of travel.

On his grandmother's death his parents, alarmed
at the disastrous effects of this *régime* of mollycoddle,
made an attempt to restore their child to a normal
condition of body and mind; they were too late.
Glinka's life was spent in combating not only real but
imaginary complaints.

His father, as was customary among landowners at that period, frequently entertained on a generous scale; his means, however, were not sufficient to permit of the provision of a permanent household orchestra, and on occasions when he desired to hold festival he borrowed the band belonging to his wife's brother, who lived but a few miles distant.

One day they played a clarinet quartet by the Finnish composer Bertrand Crusell, and this made so profound an impression on the child that, during lesson hours, his drawing-master remarked on what he was pleased to consider an undue preoccupation with music. To this the boy replied: "How can I help it? Music is my soul."

But what pleased him most was the folk-music that was rendered on festive occasions by a wind band during supper-time. To this early acquaintance with native song, suggests the composer, was due his life-long affection for this kind of melody.

At about this time Michael and his sister, Ludmilla, began receiving instruction from one Varvara Feodor-ovna Klemmer, a governess hailing from Petrograd. From her they had lessons in French, German, Russian, and Music. Her method was "mechanical," but despite this drawback her pupils made steady progress.

Young Glinka now made his first acquaintance with the violin, one of the fiddlers in his uncle's band being told off to teach him. A faulty method of holding the bow is the sole acquirement mentioned as resulting from this tuition.

A general education of far greater significance than the mere instrumental instruction was meanwhile being carried out. Listening to the band, the boy learned that if the works of well-known European composers could not oust the Russian folk-songs from their place in his affections, they were at least worthy of his esteem.

II.

At the beginning of the winter of 1817 the Glinka family went to Petrograd, and Michael entered the Pedagogical Institute, a school reserved for the aristocracy. In his Memoirs there is an amusing account of its professorial staff. The teachers in charge of the higher forms were men of liberal education, trained in Occidental Universities; those of the lower were somewhat less cultivated. Among these is mentioned one Bitton " . . . a rough Englishman, probably of the mercantile-marine class "; another was sub-Inspector Kolmakof, an amiable person whom the boys loved to " rag," and about whom they composed doggerel which Glinka set to music. The specimen quoted in the Memoirs is not without value, since it shows that even at this date the composer's sympathies were with folk rather than with art music.

At the time of the Glinkas' arrival in Petrograd the leading pianist in the capital was "Russian" Field. Michael's parents, determined to do their best for the boy, arranged that he should be taught by the

distinguished Irishman. Only three lessons had been
given, however, when Field left for Moscow, and
Glinka's piano tuition was entrusted successively to
Field's pupil Oman, Zeuner, and finally to Karl
Meyer, who proved a much more satisfactory teacher
than the others and, into the bargain, a good friend.
Violin lessons were taken under Boehm, who uttered
the famous and prophetic observation, "*Messieu
Klinka, fous ne shouerez shamais tu fiolon*."

"Despite my want of success," relates Boehm's
pupil, "I was soon able to take a place in my uncle's
orchestra." Their repertory consisted of overtures by
Cherubini and Mehul, and the symphonies of Haydn,
Mozart and Beethoven. Young Glinka determined
to prove himself worthy of his unofficial appointment
as conductor, and to this end occupied himself with
the study of the various orchestral instruments.

Life in Petrograd was favourable to his musical
development, since, besides the frequent opportunities
of hearing concerts and attending the Opera, he had the
entrée to houses in which music was seriously regarded.
During a visit to the capital his father took him to
the Lvofs', where he, like many another contemporary
musician, was profoundly impressed by the violin-play-
ing of the compóser of the Russian National Anthem.

"At the beginning of the spring of 1822, I was
introduced," record the Memoirs, "to a family in
which I became acquainted with a charming young
lady; she played the harp really well, and had a remarkable soprano voice. . . ." Desirous of rendering

2

homage, he wrote some variations on a theme from Weigl's "Swiss Family," which was a special favourite just then not only with this fascinating young person, but with society at large; he composed also some further variations for harp and piano on a theme of Mozart's, and a valse in E for piano. According to Stassof, only the harp variations were preserved.

Meanwhile his studies with Meyer were beginning to bear fruit, and on the day of his graduation, in 1822, he appeared in the programme of a school concert, playing Hummel's double piano concerto with his master.

His other work was not so successful. He made progress only in the subjects that appealed to him. Languages were in favour, and he attained a good knowledge of English, German, Latin, and Persian; French he did not care for, and consequently neglected. His apathy was the subject of much concern among his professors, and they were not slow in expressing dissatisfaction with the scant application shown by their dilatory pupil. By means, however, of certain cunning expedients, whose nature the candidate has not specified, he contrived to emerge triumphant from his final examination with the rank of Collegiate Councillor.

III.

In the ensuing autumn, following the advice of his father, who viewed the young man's poor health with some anxiety, he made the journey to the Caucasus in order to undergo a course of medicinal waters. On his way he visited the Ukraine, reaching his destination, Pyatigorsk, in the spring. The waters did not, however, produce the desired effect, and in the beginning of September the patient, by his doctor's orders, returned to his father's house in Novospasskoi, where he once more busied himself with musical pursuits. Renewing his experiments with his uncle's orchestra, he strove to familiarize himself, aided by its members, with the functions of the various instruments and with the repertory of the band as a whole. Apparently his status as pupil of the individual did not interfere with his authority as conductor.

In March, 1826, he was able to return to Petrograd and on his father's recommendation he accepted a secretarial post in the Ministry of Ways and Communications. This he did not retain for long; the work, though light, proved distasteful. Indirectly the appointment had a profitable result, being instrumental in securing the friendship of Count Sivers, an enthusiastic and influential amateur.

As was natural, on returning to the capital he lost no time in seeking out his former teacher, Karl Meyer. The latter, on being invited to resume his tuition, refused to undertake this on the previous terms: "You have too much talent for me to give you lessons," he said; "come to me daily as a friend, and we will make music together." Availing himself of this genial invitation, Glinka was frequently at the Meyers', occasionally playing four-handed arrangements of the classics with the elder of his friend's two sisters.

It happened at this time that "the famous contrapuntist" Mueller visited Petrograd, but Glinka failed to come in touch with him. "Who knows ? It was no doubt for the best. This severe German counterpoint is not the sort of thing that lends wings to the imagination." Thus the composer of "Russlan and Ludmilla."

His friendship with Count Sivers brought intercourse with many musical families. Prince Galitsin, Count Vielhorsky, and the famous Baroness Krudener's brother were his associates at this time, and at their gatherings music was the chief attraction.

He had already made a number of attempts at vocal composition. These had not been very successful, and, in order to improve his knowledge of the voice as instrument, he began a course of lessons with Belloli, a well-known Italian singer. He continued at the same time to profit by the advice of Meyer, and presently succeeded in completing a string quartet in D major, an essay which failed however to increase his self-confidence as a composer.

Shortly after this he addressed himself with greater success to the composition of the Allegro of a sonata in D minor for piano and viola, and for the celebration of the betrothal of his niece he wrote a set of piano variations on the popular Italian air, "Benedetta sia la madre," this being his first published work. Before leaving Smolensk, whither he had journeyed for the ceremony, he composed some choruses and an aria with piano and double-bass accompaniment, in commemoration of the death of Alexander I. and the accession of Nicholas. With this work he expressed himself satisfied "notwithstanding some blemishes."

This was followed by some songs, a chorus "On the Death of a Hero," and an aria for baritone, part of which was used many years later in "Russlan and Ludmilla." Not long after came another contribution to that opera, an air sung to the composer by a member of the staff of the Persian Embassy; in this air originated the delightful Persian chorus of the third act. Small "romances" formed the greater part of his output at this epoch, and they, as he himself admits. represent his romantic or sentimental period. Such specimens as "The Moon shines on the Cemetery," and the music to Baryatinsky's "Do not needlessly torment me," are doubtless what Goncharof's Adouef* would have described as "sincere outpourings."

About this time occurred an event which, remote as it may seem from the chief concerns of Glinka's life, had considerable bearing upon his subsequent activities. In the spring of 1827 a highly placed acquaintance, aware of a desire on the part of Glinka's father to improve his financial resources by means of speculation, placed before him a scheme, advanced a considerable amount of money—apparently on the security of "an unblemished reputation"—and was able to repay himself handsomely when the time arrived to share the proceeds. Through this sudden

* "A Common Story."

change in his father's position Glinka found himself relieved of any necessity of following a remunerative calling, and threw himself forthwith into what has been described as a life of " frenzied dilettantism." He joined his friends in a series of musical revels of which he gives the fullest particulars in the Memoirs.

Towards the end of August, 1829, they organized an excursion on the Chernaya river. Together with Prince Galitsin and T. M. Tolstoi (later known as critic by the *nom de guerre* of " Rostislaf ") they embarked in boats decorated with Venetian lamps. On one they carried the trumpeters of the Household Cavalry; on the prow of another was placed a small piano, at which Glinka presided as conductor. Tolstoi was exceedingly successful in the Venetian barcarolle " Da brava Catina," and Boieldieu's chorus, " Sonnez, sonnez, cors et musettes," from " La Dame Blanche," also figured in the programme. Between the songs the trumpeters played a flourish. The proceedings were fully reported in the *Northern Bee*, and " this first success encouraged us to seek further entertainment of a like nature."

Their next enterprise took the form of a complimentary performance to Prince Kochoubey, president of the Imperial Council. Glinka, one of a party of sixteen, which included Meyer the pianist, attired in the costume and wig of Donna Anna, gave a selection from Mozart's " Don Juan." Entertainments were subsequently given at Tsarskoe Selo, when Ivanof, the great operatic singer, performed a serenade of

Glinka's composition, and also at Princess Stroganof's country house at Marino, where the composer undertook the rôle of Figaro in "The Barber."

IV.

This sort of life was not to be indulged in with impunity by anyone of so frail a constitution as Glinka. He had already been troubled, a year or two back, with àn affection of the eyes, and at the close of 1828 he at last realized that his health was not equal to the strain he was putting upon it. For some little time he struggled on, seeking by means of various treatments to avoid a breakdown, until in 1829 Dr. Spindler, discovering a "whole quadrille of disorders," impressed upon the patient the necessity of spending at least three years in a warm climate.

Hence his departure, on Friday, April 25th, 1830, for Italy. As *compagnon de voyage* he was accompanied by Ivanof, who had been granted leave of absence from the Imperial Chapel by Feodor Lvof, its director. Together they visited in turn Dresden, Leipzig, and Frankfort, from whence they explored the Rhine. It was as much a musical pilgrimage as a pursuit of health, and the two friends added to the interest of the journey by visiting the opera houses of the towns through which they passed. Continuing their travels they proceeded via Switzerland to Milan.

Glinka had made provision for improving his

technique while in Italy, and had been furnished with a letter of introduction to Basili, the director of the Milan Conservatoire. With him the young Russian began to take lessons in composition. But Basili's methods were so austere that they failed altogether to appeal to so haphazard a student, and the studies speedily came to a close.

The chronicle of his life in Italy would fill many pages. For the present purpose it should suffice to record that during his sojourn he made many friends, that he composed a number of small piano pieces— chiefly variations on themes of Rossini, Donizetti and Bellini—and that in the end he terminated his visit to the South because his long absence from his native land had begun to make him feel homesick.

But his complaint was not the ordinary kind of nostalgia. Glinka had become convinced that writing in the Italian manner did not fulfil his artistic needs. He had begun to feel that in order to express himself he must find some other means than the "*sentimento brillante*" of Italian music. The Memoirs give a hint at this stage that the germ of Russian musical nationalism was now ready for cultivation. "Without a doubt our sad Russian songs are children of the North, with certain Oriental characteristics. . . ." Such words might well have been uttered for the express purpose of heralding Glinka's two great operas, so completely do they foreshadow their substance.

It was not, however, at the moment of leaving Italy, but during a somewhat protracted homeward journey, that the idea of composing a national opera entered his mind. Passing through Vienna, where he conceived a theme that appears in "A Life for the Tsar," he arrived in the late autumn of 1833 in Berlin. Here he was introduced to Siegfried Dehn, a well-known teacher, and curator of the musical section of the Royal Library. Under his guidance Glinka began his first serious course of study, which lasted for five months. "He made me write fugues in three or four parts . . . on themes from well-known compositions."

Fortified by the consciousness of an improved technique, he set himself to compose a number of songs on Russian texts and a *pot-pourri* of folk-songs for piano. In the meantime the desire to write a national opera had so completely taken possession of him, that he had already composed the music subsequently used for the Orphan's Song, and part of the overture for "A Life for the Tsar."

His state of mind is well reflected in a letter to an unnamed friend, dated from Berlin:

"I have a project in view . . ." it runs; "this is not perhaps the moment to make a complete avowal; perhaps if I told you everything your face might wear an expression of incredulity. I may as well tell you at any rate that you may expect to find me not a little altered . . . probably you will be astonished at the change that has taken place in me since last we met in St. Petersburg. Shall I confess ? . . . I am in hopes of contributing to our national repertory a work of an ambitious kind. It may not prove, I must at once admit, a *chef-d'œuvre*, but at least it will not be a failure ! . . . The most important thing is to make a good choice of subject. It must be national . . . by virtue not only of its literary material but of its music as well. I am anxious that my fellow-countrymen shall, when listening to it, feel that they are at home, that the foreigner shall not take me for an upstart who struts about as might a crow in peacock's plumage. . . ."

V.

On hearing of the death of his father Glinka resolved to return home, and in April, 1834, he set out on the journey to Novospasskoi, travelling via Tilsit. He describes home life as having proved pleasant and peaceful, but as he remained barely a month one supposes that the desire for musical company was stronger than his love of quietude. He had indeed already thought of going abroad once again, and his departure for Moscow, where he hoped to rejoin his friend Melgounof, was to have been the first stage of a longer journey. Despite the constantly recurring thoughts of the projected opera (for which he had not yet succeeded in finding a libretto), he only awaited his passport to pay another visit to Berlin. The document duly arrived, but in the meantime the intending pilgrim had found an object of worship nearer home.

Her name was Maria Petrovna Ivanovna. Her sister was the wife of his friend Stuneyef, at whose house in Petrograd Glinka met the young woman. For the best of reasons he now chose the capital as the centre of his activities, and by so doing brought two extremely important matters to a head. In May, 1835, Maria Petrovna became his wife. During the courtship he came in touch with a circle of intellectuals who were accustomed to meet at the house of the poet Joukovsky, then holding a position in the royal family. Among them were Pushkin, Viazemsky, Odoievsky, Vielhorsky, and Gogol, who on one occasion read his play " The Matchmaker," afterwards used by Moussorgsky as the foundation of his unfinished opera of that name.

At one of their gatherings Joukovsky suggested a plot, offering to write the book of the proposed opera and actually completing some verses. The subject was now decided upon. Ivan Soussanin, credited by historians with having sacrificed himself to save his sovereign, and already the hero of a work by Cavos, was to be the central figure. Cavos's title was discarded, and that eventually given to the work was " A Life for the Tsar." Joukovsky's only contribution will be found in the Trio of the Epilogue.

Joukovsky's reason for abandoning the promised work was that he had no leisure for additional labours. He was able, however, to procure the services of the Tsarevich's secretary, Baron Rosen, an erudite German littérateur. One imagines that at the moment of this choice the flame of Russian nationalism can hardly have been burning as brightly as it did on the occasions when the circle of young poets met in Joukovsky's salon. Rosen has rightly been blamed for the poor quality of his libretto. At the same time one must allow that circumstances were all against the proper accomplishment of his task.

Having settled the plan of his opera, Glinka took the step which, as may be gleaned from his correspondence at the time, he hoped would bring him life-long happiness. This hope, as we shall see, was not to be realized. It seems a little strange, even in these circumstances, that the very date of his wedding should afterwards have been effaced from his memory. " At the close of April, 1835, about the 25th or 26th," he wrote some twenty years later, " I was married."

Early in May he betook himself with his bride to Novospasskoi, and lost no time in setting to work on his opera. During a journey to Novgorod he composed its famous nuptial chorus in $\frac{5}{4}$ time.

Conjugal felicity seemed now to the young husband to be the one thing needful to inspire him. " The work progressed splendidly," runs the autobiographical account; ". . . every morning I sat at my table and wrote about six pages in small score. . . . In the evening, sitting on the sofa, surrounded by the whole family and on occasion by a few intimate friends as well, I was for the most part oblivious of what was going on around me. I was wholly absorbed in my work."

VI.

While such a generous flow of ideas was wholly favourable to the spontaneity of Glinka's music, it was by no means a boon to the unfortunate Rosen. More than once it fell to him to reverse the customary procedure by writing words to music. The Joukovsky circle were highly amused at the method imposed upon the Baron, and chaffed him about the varied assortment of verses alleged by them to be ready in his pocket awaiting the demands of Glinka's abundant inspiration.

In the winter of 1835-36, when the opera was approaching completion, it was privately rehearsed in sections by a number of artists and amateurs who were interested spectators of Glinka's labours. Among them were his friend Petrof, Mlle. Vorobief, who afterwards married that great singer, and Shemayef. Gedeonof, the director of the opera, was greatly perturbed by their frequent attendance at rehearsals held in the smoke-laden atmosphere of a smallish room which, he contended, could not fail to be detrimental to their voices. He made no objection, however, when invited to attend a rehearsal of the first act, which took place at Count Vielhorsky's house in March, 1836. It was a rehearsal not merely for the artists but also for the composer. Glinka received a number of excellent suggestions from his host, as well as from Prince Odoievsky, and Karl Meyer.

The composer had already made some unsuccessful representations to the Directorate of the Imperial Theatres with regard to the staging of his opera. Following upon Gedeonof's participation in this audition, however, their decision was reversed, and the opera was put into rehearsal, Cavos, who had been one of Glinka's strongest advocates, being in charge.

Preparations were carried on throughout the summer of 1836, and during these Glinka was able to note with satisfaction that his opera was likely to produce the effect he desired. The orchestra appeared enraptured with the music, and made no attempt to conceal their feelings. A tribute of a different kind came from the Emperor, who, being present at one of the rehearsals, consented to accept the dedication of the new opera.

At length all was ready. On Friday, November 27th, 1836, " A Life for the Tsar " was given its first public performance.

" It is impossible to describe the feelings I experienced on that occasion, particularly before the performance began. I occupied a box in the second balcony; the first was reserved for the State officials and for the families of the Court entourage. My wife and relations were with me in the box.

" The first act was a great success, being warmly and vigorously applauded. . . . The Orphan's Song, the duet between Vorobief and Petrof, the quartet and the Poles' scene, were particularly successful. . . . In the fourth act, the chorus, enacting the part of the Polish soldiers, fell upon Petrof with such rage that they tore his shirt, and he was obliged to defend himself in real earnest. . . ."

In the diary of Glinka's friend Nestor Kukolnik, the poet and dramatist, the following appears: "It was an epoch-making event in the history of Russian artistic accomplishment. The Russian theatre was witness of an indescribable enthusiasm; and not merely enthusiasm but emotion. I myself saw many men and women weeping, and even the Tsar had tears in his eyes. Misha (Glinka), ill with excitement and happiness, cried like a child on the homeward drive."

After the performance the Emperor sent for the composer, shook him by the hand, and talked with him about the opera for some little time. The other members of the Imperial family also paid the most flattering tributes to the music. Shortly after this he received from the Emperor a magnificent diamond and topaz ring in return for his dedication of the opera, and two days after the performance word was brought him that a post in the Imperial Chapel, which he had hitherto vainly endeavoured to obtain, was now to be given to him.

The chorus of praise that greeted "A Life for the Tsar" was not allowed by the critics, however, to pass unchallenged. Some there were who complained that there was nothing novel in Glinka's music; others, contemptuously referring to the fragment of folksong which the composer had overheard from a cab-driver and had given prominence in his opera, described it as "*la musique des cochers*." One Krapovitsky

complained that the composer had borrowed from
the Russians but had given nothing to the rest of the
world, "the result—nonsense." Thadeus Bulgarin,
in the *Northern Bee*, replied to an observation made
by Prince Odoievsky—that Glinka had endowed music
with a new element—by asserting that it was impossible to invent any novel means of musical expression, since everything already existed.

To say that Russian musical criticism was in those
days not altogether free from bias would be completely
to understate the case. Even in those rare instances
where the power of judgment existed at all, it was
entirely subjugated when occasion demanded to the
desire, arising out of personal motives, to condemn.
It would hardly be fair, therefore, to place this opera
among the many instances in which critical opinion
has been entirely at fault. One need only endorse
Stassof's observation that "A Life for the Tsar"
marks an epoch in the history of Russian art by
pointing out that if the music of this opera has, during
the eighty odd years since its composition, lost some
of its emotional power, one has but to compare it with
contemporary products to realize the genius of its
creator.

VII.

It was not long before Glinka began to make plans
for the writing of a second opera. On January 1st,
1837, he took over his new duties in the Imperial

Chapel, and for some little time busied himself with the arrangement of his work there. But that once settled, the desire to repeat his success on the operatic stage became paramount. From sources other than his own promptings he received plenty of encouragement. The first suggestion of the subject of " Russlan and Ludmilla " came from Prince Shakovsky. Then Pushkin, the author of the poem, announced at one of Joukovsky's evenings his wish to make certain alterations in it which would render it suitable for the musical purpose. Eventually it was agreed that the poet should prepare a libretto. In addition the composer's new ambition had been, in a way, anticipated by the Tsar, who remarked to Glinka's friend Stuneyef, at a patriotic concert at which an excerpt from " A Life for the Tsar " was performed: " Glinka is a great master; it would be a pity were he to remain satisfied with this single opera." Finally the composer received from the eminent marine painter Aivazovsky three Tartar melodies, entirely suitable as music for the chosen subject.

The composing of " Russlan and Ludmilla " was carried out under far less propitious conditions than those prevailing with the previous work. In the first place Pushkin's death (in 1837), in a duel, put an end to a poetic partnership which had appeared quite ideal. Secondly, things were not going at all well at home. His wife, from whom he had expected such happiness, had turned out to be a woman who cared for little else than the outward signs of her inward frivolity.

Already, during the composition of " A Life for the Tsar," the disenchanted husband had observed disconcerting evidences of Maria Petrovna's indifference to the things that matter.　Her complaint that he was "wasting too much money on music-paper " came as a decided shock to the young composer, flushed as he was with the consciousness of his inspiration.　On another occasion when, as comment on Pushkin's death, she uttered the opinion that all artists came to a bad end, Glinka was provoked to make the wrathful answer that whilst not claiming a superior wisdom he, at any rate, would not risk his life, as Pushkin had done, for his wife's good name.　In the end the separation which had long appeared inevitable was agreed upon, and Glinka, vowing that marriage, like many other matters, was to be regarded as " counterpoint: opposition, contrary motion . . ." began to learn the meaning of real unhappiness.

Towards Easter, 1838, he travelled to Little-Russia, for the purpose of seeking in that happy hunting-ground of the choral director some new voices for the Imperial Chapel.　Returning with nineteen boys and three men—one of them, discovered at Kief, was Gulak-Artemovsky, a singer who soon justified Glinka's confidence—he received for this service a grant of fifteen hundred roubles.　He did not long continue his work at the Chapel.　His retirement, partly due to his bad health, took place at the end of 1839.

Consequent upon the lamented death of Pushkin, Glinka was obliged to search for a new librettist.

The subject was naturally retained. It was impossible, however, that any other hand than the poet's could deal with the original as would have Pushkin. To make matters infinitely worse, Glinka committed the grievous error of dividing the work among several librettists. The first step was to invite Bakhtourin to sketch out a plan. Bakhtourin, a bibulous member of the literary circle surrounding Glinka, took his task so lightly that he devoted no more than a quarter of an hour to its accomplishment. The composer, by no means satisfied, subjected the plan to a considerable modification. He then approached his friend Kukolnik, and Michael the brother of Gedeonof the operatic director, and invited them to supply the text. Further, a portion of the first act is the work of a Captain Shirkof, and the verses of Finn's ballad are by Glinka's school-friend Markovich.

Little wonder, then, that the result, to use the words of that vigorous critic César Cui, is somewhat kaleidoscopic. The music was composed "by fits and starts," the interruptions being due partly to physical and partly to mental causes. In the spring of 1840, spent at Novospasskoi, he was constantly ailing, and for a long time after the disastrous termination of his married life he was exceedingly unhappy.

But while the opera did not make much progress, there is a work of no small significance that belongs originally to this period, and lends to it a special importance. This is the incidental music to his friend

Kukolnik's drama "Prince Kholmsky," a work of such great charm that it is difficult to account for its neglect.

VIII.

Glinka has himself recorded that his life at this period was exceedingly monotonous, and that the tedium was difficult to endure. Considering his despondency during its composition, the score of "Russlan" is an extraordinary achievement. Its charm and grace might easily have led one to suppose that this, and not " A Life for the Tsar," was composed during the happiest period of his life. "If only the fates will bestow a smile upon me," wrote the composer in a letter dated March 1st, 1841, "I feel sure that ere long my poor 'Russlan' will be completed."

Not until a year later was this accomplished. In the spring of 1842 the score was placed before Gedeonof, who recompensed the composer for the initial rebuff administered in respect of " A Life for the Tsar " by accepting the new opera without demur, and on terms extremely favourable to the composer's pocket. Preparations were forthwith begun.

But if the smiles solicited from the fates were vouchsafed, they soon turned to frowns. The rehearsals were carried out under most unfavourable conditions. There was a decided lack of discipline in the orchestra; the scenery left much to be desired; Mme. Petrof fell ill, and had to be replaced at the eleventh hour by an inexperienced singer whose sole claim to the sudden distinction appears to have been that she was the unfortunate Petrova's namesake; and finally the sting of Bulgarin's *Northern Bee* was felt in an article which sought to make mischief between the composer and his artists.

There were, of course, other reasons that the first performance of " Russlan and Ludmilla," which took place on November 27th, 1842, could not be expected to provoke the enthusiasm which had prevailed on a November evening of six years before—a scene so tersely and yet so comprehensively described by Kukolnik. The heroic and realistic nature of the stage happenings in " A Life for the Tsar " would themselves be quite sufficient without music to arouse at least a keen interest. The subject of " Russlan and Ludmilla," elaborated by Pushkin before he had developed the true folk-lore manner, is one which makes much bigger demands upon the imagination; the music, moreover, is greatly in advance of that of " A Life for the Tsar," and the Oriental element, introduced in obedience to the requirements of the text, was an absolute novelty in Russia at that time.

Surviving accounts of the first performance vary so much that it is difficult to determine the degree of success achieved by some of the more popular numbers, and the extent of public and critical disappointment with the opera as a whole. One writer dwells upon the hisses that greeted the work, another on the applause. Count Vielhorsky, then engaged on a

setting of Pushkin's "The Gipsies,"* appears to have
been prompted by jealousy to condemn the work.
At one of the rehearsals he spoke harshly of it; on
the first night he left the theatre before the performance was over, and at supper, at the house of Count
Kutuzof, remarked to Glinka that it was "*un opera
manqué.*" It was soon freely rumoured that attendance on "Russlan" nights had been adopted as a
disciplinary measure by commanding officers. The
fact is that St. Petersburg musical society was divided
into two classes, advocates and opponents of Italian
music.

"Russlan and Ludmilla," in spite of this conflict
of opinion, possibly because of it, enjoyed a "run"
of thirty-two performances, and of twenty-one in the
following season. In the end, however, Italian music
won the day, and nothing more was heard for quite
a long time of Glinka's second opera.

IX.

Much of the year following (1843) was spent at
Novospasskoi; but in the winter Glinka returned to
the capital, and paid occasional visits to the scene of
his lost battle, listening to the performances of Rubini,
Tamburini, and Viardot-Garcia. During the period
following upon the shock of disappointment Glinka
composed only a few songs. He felt the need of a

* The subject of Rakhmaninof's opera "Aleko."

change, and decided once more to leave his native land for a warmer clime. By June, 1844, he had made up his mind to go to Spain, and, having paid a brief visit to his mother, he proceeded to Smolensk and thence, via Warsaw, to Berlin. Here he spent five days with Dehn who, as the composer records, was exceedingly pleased with the final Trio from "A Life for the Tsar." Nothing is said, however, as to the German's reception of the other score.

From Berlin he travelled via Brussels, where he experienced the joys of the annual "Kermesse," to Paris. Life in the French city at first somewhat bored the composer. But Glinka soon found a kindred spirit in Hector Berlioz, who at that time was also suffering from the neglect of his native public. This acquaintanceship delayed for a time the journey Glinka had determined on making to Spain. Berlioz was about to pay his first visit to Russia, and hastened to pay a compliment to Glinka by writing an encomiastic newspaper article on the Russian composer, and by including in the programmes of his "Concerts-Monstres" at the Champs Elysées Circus some excerpts from "A Life for the Tsar" and "Russlan and Ludnilla." These did not meet with any notable success, and a further concert which Glinka himself gave, supported by Prince Galitsin and attended by all the Russian colony and a considerable number of Parisians, brought him only a *succès d'estime* and a loss of fifteen hundred francs. By some three or four exceedingly favourable notices, one of them from the pen of

Berlioz, Glinka was, however, amply repaid. Writing
to Kukolnik in April, 1845, he requested him to have
inserted in the *Northern Bee* a translation of Berlioz'
article as evidence of the great Frenchman's esteem
for the exiled prophet.

These concerts over, Glinka bethought himself once
more of the Spanish project. A letter to his mother
about this time records his desire to apply himself
again to a great work, the inspiration for which he
hoped to find in the national melodies of Spain. In
another, dated May 24th, he acknowledges the receipt
of funds from his brother and announces his impending
departure for the South. "Paris," he writes, "is a
terrible place for one's pocket. Money, money,
money. Here the whole world seems to revolve upon
it." His letters are to be addressed "A don Miguel
de Glinka—posta restanta en Madrid."

The letter to Kukolnik, above quoted, contains a
reference to the ambitions which the visit to Spain
was expected to realize. "I am in hopes of enriching
my répertoire with a few (and if health permits, with
several) concert pieces for orchestra under the generic
title of "Fantaisies pittoresques." Continuing, he
explains that in his view the formalism of the symphony
prevents it from being appreciated by the majority
of the concert-going public. Variations fatigue the
ear too much. He feels that there is a need for a
new kind of concert-piece accessible equally to the
erudite musician and to the ordinary public. He
explains that a beginning has been made by adding

a Coda to Chernomor's March (from "Russlan and Ludmilla"). "I hope while in Spain to compose such Fantasias—the originality of the indigenous tunes should furnish me with the necessary material, especially as hitherto no one has exploited them."

Spending the summer in Valladolid, Glinka occupied himself in busily searching out these melodies. In this he was aided by Castilla, a celebrated exponent of the guitar. Through the latter he procured the themes of both the "Jota Aragonesa" and the "Summer Night in Madrid."

Writing from Pampluna (the birthplace of Sarasate) to his mother, he concludes an account of his researches with the regret that "as with us, musicians here are slaves to the Italian tradition."

Glinka was well pleased with the conditions of life in Spain, and he remained there until June, 1847, when he turned his face homeward again. He then settled in Smolensk, where he lived with his married sister Ludmilla (Mme. Shestakof). Here he wrote a few songs, but was prevented by ill-health from making any considerable addition to his works. To pass away the time his sister read to him, and gathered around him a few favoured friends, with whom he played "preference." This quiet, homely life lasted until January, 1848. Two months later, the desire for travel having returned, he began preparations for a journey to Paris. Owing, however, to the disturbances in France, his passport was refused, and an alteration of plans was necessitated. Until 1852 he lived in Warsaw.

He revised the "Jota Aragonesa," and also the "Night in Madrid," whilst in the Polish capital. The local Censor, applying his energies in a constructive direction, proposed to him certain poems as texts for songs, and read to the composer "the great works of many Russian and other authors, Shakespeare in particular."

But these were not the choicest fruits of this period.

Chancing one day to hear at a village wedding a nuptial song and a traditional dance measure (Kamarinskaya) simultaneously, he conceived the idea of incorporating them in an orchestral fantasia under the name "Wedding Song and Dance." "How astonishingly original," writes Tchaikovsky of Glinka to his patroness Nadejda von Meck, in 1880, "is his 'Kamarinskaya,' from which all Russian composers who followed him (including myself) continue to this day to borrow contrapuntal and harmonic combinations directly they have to develop a Russian dance tune ! . . ."

X.

In June, 1852, Glinka continued the so long interrupted journey to Paris, making a short stay in Berlin. He spent most of his time there with Dehn, but his meeting with Meyerbeer deserves mention. The Western composer expressed his regret that while Glinka's reputation had spread far and wide, his works were very little known. "That," replied Glinka, "is not strange, for I am not in the habit of hawking my wares."

Writing to Kukolnik, from Paris, towards the end of 1852, Glinka directed his friend to address him in Madrid. The next letter opens thus: "*Rien n'est sûr que l'imprévu.*" Having got as far as Toulouse, his old enemy ill-health had obliged him to abandon the journey. As soon as he was able, he returned to Paris. A few days later he was writing his impressions of the Louvre to his compatriot Serof, the composer.

During September he began work on a new symphonic enterprise which was to have taken the shape of a "Ukrainian Symphony"; its subject was based on Gogol's epic novel "Taras Bulba"—a work that has inspired more than one Russian composer. Only the first part of the opening Allegro and a small part of the second were composed, Glinka putting the work on one side because he felt himself unable to defeat a tendency to develop his themes in the German manner.

Glinka remained in France until the spring of 1854. He appears during this sojourn to have made a wide study of both the literature and the zoology of several lands. The Jardin des Plantes was a favourite haunt.

Towards the end of March he wrote to Mme. Shestakof announcing that in all probability this would be his last letter from Paris. Ere the treaty was signed in which England and France engaged jointly to prosecute a war against Russia, Glinka was in Brussels, and by the middle of the month he was once more making music with Dehn.

Having called at Warsaw he made his way to Tsarskoe Selo. Here he lived with Mme. Shestakof, who urged him to begin writing the Memoirs to which we have so frequently had recourse. At Tsarskoe Selo he received visits from many celebrated Russian musicians. Among them were Lvof, Serof (who had a great affection for " Russlan "), Dmitri Stassof, Villebois, and Dargomijsky, who brought with him from time to time his opera " Russalka."

His visitors were not all, however, of the sterner sex. He saw a great deal of the eminent singer Mme. Leonof; and receiving from Shakovsky the suggestion of setting Kukolnik's " The Bigamist," he began to consider this operatic undertaking, having in mind the intention to arrange for a prominent rôle for Leonova. He proposed also to utilize some of the Little-Russian themes which had been collected for " Taras Bulba." But by the time the libretto reached him he had been once more stricken down with illness.

XI.

During the ensuing winter he received word from Oulibishef, the biographer of Mozart, that a young man named Balakiref would call upon him. The founder of the " New Russian School " was quickly recognized by the " father of Russian Opera " as likely to attain the position he ultimately won; in Glinka's opinion the future leader of the Petrograd " Five " had views more closely resembling his own than those of any other musician among the rising generation. He counted upon young Balakiref to keep alive the Nationalist tradition when his own labours should be over.

Despite the prominent place occupied by his proposed third opera in Glinka's thoughts at this moment, his attention was now suddenly turned in an entirely different direction. He had long wished to know something more of church music, and especially of the constitution of the ecclesiastical modes. With the intention of studying this question with Dehn he took, in April, 1856, what proved to be his last journey abroad.

Under Dehn's guidance Glinka applied himself assiduously to his new researches. But they were not to be brought to a practical issue. Meyerbeer, wishing to do honour to the great Russian composer, arranged a brilliant Court concert at which the Trio from " A Life for the Tsar " was the principal attraction. Glinka received a tremendous ovation, which he described in a letter to his sister, Mme. Shestakof, under date January 27-15th, 1857. It was the last she ever received from him. When leaving the concert her brother caught a chill, and on February 15th breathed his last. His body was brought to Petrograd and was deposited in the cemetery of the Alexander Nevsky Monastery.

Soon after his burial a monument was erected on

the tomb, embellished with a medallion bearing a profile portrait of the composer. On the fortieth anniversary of the production of " A Life for the Tsar," a bust was placed in the Maryinsky Theatre, and at this moment his devoted sister set on foot a scheme for the publication of the scores of his operatic works.

In 1885, Glinka's birthday was celebrated by the unveiling of an elaborate memorial at Smolensk, which bears on. its four sides the names of his principal compositions and favourite themes from the two operas, the " Prince Kholmsky " music and the ballad ".The Midnight Review." A monument was erected in Petrograd in 1906.

The prophet has also been honoured in another land than his own. In 1900 the house in Berlin in which Glinka died was rebuilt, and was furnished as a museum, the Tsar presenting a monument, consisting of a bust of the composer of " Russlan and Ludmilla " flanked by the figures of its hero and heroine.

A memorial of an entirely different but equally enduring kind was inaugurated in 1884 when Belayef, the founder of the non-commercial publishing firm, distributed by proxy the first of the Glinka Prizes which are now handed annually, on the anniversary of the production of the two operas, to the composers of the best orchestral and chamber works published during the past year. It would be difficult to conceive a more suitable means of perpetuating the memory of a master who fully realized that his work was not the fruit but the seed.

PART II

GLINKA AS OPERATIC COMPOSER

"A LIFE FOR THE TSAR"

I.

To appreciate the full value of Glinka's operatic compositions it is necessary to bear in mind that they are something more than merely a culmination of the previous attempts at an expression of nationalism. The subject of his first essay in dramatic music, " A Life for the Tsar," had, as we are aware, already been used by the Italian Cavos. And this was by no means the sole effort that had been made to introduce the element of nationalism into the Russian Opera.

But none of the innovators prior to Glinka had done more than avail himself of subjects pertaining to the history and folk-lore of Russia; some of them, indeed, had actually employed a foreign tongue as the literary expression of their nationalism. As to the music, that was written by men whose memory was so well stocked with reminiscences of the alien music that since Peter the Great's time had always been sure of a welcome in Russian cities, that they were incapable of controlling their pens. Tradition had hold of their wrists. The snatches of folk-song that occur in these operas are nothing more than decorative fragments pinned on to a garment. In " A Life for the Tsar " one notices certain "Italianisms " that are to be regarded as a blemish upon that work. But in Glinka's case the garment really is Russian.

It would be unfair to deride the attempts of Glinka's forerunners. Not only were they themselves steeped in the foreign tradition, but the public addressed by them would have taken no interest whatever in an endeavour to dignify Opera by means of the employment of a realistic plot and relevant music. To realize what the late eighteenth and early nineteenth century composer had to contend with, it suffices to recall that Cavos found it necessary to fit a "happy ending " to his version of the story of Soussanin, the hero of " A Life for the Tsar."

With Glinka began the tradition of true nationalism in Russian Music. Comparing " A Life for the Tsar " with another example of patriotic opera, "William Tell," M. Bellaigue reminds us that in the latter the emancipation of Switzerland is celebrated in a French type of opera written by an Italian. In Glinka's work there is nothing of this kind at which to cavil. The composer was sufficiently Russian to suffer from nostalgia when surrounded by Italian musical influences during his first visit to the South. His plot, it is true, is based upon an episode which is discredited by some of the historians. But the episode is garnered from an epoch which may well be considered as one of the most important pages in the history of Russia.

Finally, Glinka's music is largely Russian and Polish in character; the intrusion of passages bearing a Western complexion is sometimes attributed to the composer's long sojourn abroad; but if he had never left his native land the history of music in Russia might easily have accounted for this.

Glinka, in taking up the challenge of Dehn, his teacher, "Go and write Russian music," scorned to follow in the footsteps of those who had been satisfied with merely stringing together a number of popular tunes. To the Russian listener the music of " A Life for the Tsar " was for the most part unfamiliar, yet it had just the effect desired by Glinka when he spoke of making his fellow-countrymen feel at home. The music is rarely the actual music of the people; it is in its resemblance to that music that its power lies. It appealed to the Russian of the 'thirties as appeals the sound of conversation in his own tongue to the exile. He may not be able to hear the conversation itself: probably he prefers that that should not reach him; the sound is just what he needs and is enough.

The text of " A Life for the Tsar " is very far from being merely the narrative of a picturesque and perhaps apocryphal episode derived from the chronicles of Russian history. It refers to a number of personages whose existence is an established fact. Whether the central figure is fictitious or not hardly matters. A high light is thrown by the opera upon the character of Soussanin, and the reflected figure is that of loyalty. Small wonder that no national festival is considered

4

complete without a performance of " A Life for the Tsar "; nor is it strange that this item in a series of ceremonies is not only the culminating event, but arouses the greatest enthusiasm.

II.

The period of Russian history ensuing on the death of Ivan the Terrible, and lasting until the accession of young Michael Romanof in 1613, is known to historians as the Time of Trouble. The trouble was at its height during the interim between the last years of Boris Godounof and the moment at which the occurrences chronicled in " A Life for the Tsar " took place. Russia's enemies at this time included, besides the Tatars, the Swedes, the Poles, and the two Pretenders whose insurrectionary endeavours have been so exhaustively dealt with by Mérimée in " Les Faux Démétrius." Their following was largely Polish. At the opening of the opera the Poles, hearing that the Muscovites have elected the young Russian noble as Tsar at the very moment when their own efforts were to have been crowned with success, determine to make a final effort to overthrow the Empire. They advance on Moscow with the object of capturing the person of the newly elected monarch. It is on this state of affairs that Glinka's curtain rises.

The first act takes place in the village in which Ivan Soussanin, a humble but heroic peasant, dwells with his daughter Antonida, and Vanya, his adopted son.

The peasants are celebrating, a little prematurely, the end of the struggle with their country's enemies; Antonida is gazing with rapture in the direction from which her gallant lover Sobinin is expected to approach the village on his return from the war. But her father is oppressed with a fear that all is not yet well. When Sobinin arrives, however, Soussanin is reassured by the news that a Tsar has been nominated, and gives his consent to the marriage of his daughter with the warrior.

The second act, like that of "Boris Godounof," transports us to Poland. The Polish nobles, confident of victory, are holding high revel. But towards the close of the act a messenger arrives from the front bringing news of a retreat and of the recent election of a Tsar.

The background of the third act is humble, but it strikes a truer note of patriotism. In Soussanin's izba, or cabin, we see in progress, during its first part, a general rejoicing in which a chorus of peasants, Soussanin, his adopted son Vanya, and the lovers participate. But the festal scene is interrupted by sounds of a disturbance outside, and Vanya, going to the window of the izba, sees a band of Polish soldiers approaching. A moment later they burst into the cabin. They are on their way to Moscow, whence they reckon on bringing back a royal prisoner. But they are uncertain of the road, and command the peasant Soussanin to act as their guide. The brave man, perceiving the danger that threatens his sovereign, resolves in an instant to dissemble. He will lead the Poles astray. Agreeing to accompany them he finds

an opportunity of divulging his plan to Vanya, whom
he bids ride at full gallop to the Tsar's retreat so that
the attack may be forestalled. Soussanin then departs
with the Poles. Antonida's young women companions
enter singing a nuptial chorus, and are amazed to find
the bride prostrate with grief at the appalling turn
events have taken. On Sobinin's arrival he hears
what has taken place, and at once organizes a pursuit.

The fourth act is divided into three scenes. The
first is not usually included in performances of the opera.
In it Sobinin and his friends are seen hunting in vain
for traces of the raiders and their guide. The second
shows us Vanya's arrival at the monastery at Kostroma, in which the young Romanof is housed. He
has ridden his steed to death and has been obliged
to complete the journey on foot. He is in pretty bad
case, but is able to summon sufficient strength to warn
the Tsar's entourage. There is again a change of
scene, which reveals the Polish band being led step
by step, Soussanin at their head, into a marshy forest
to which night and thickly falling snow lend an ever
intensifying obscurity. Presently they stop for the
night. Soussanin, realizing that his end is near, scorns
to spend his last hours in sleep, and keeps vigil for
the approaching dawn that will surely be his last.
When the storm is at its height the Poles begin to
suspect their betrayal. Soussanin temporizes for a
little, but at the first flush of dawn he triumphantly
proclaims his victory over the enemies of his Emperor.
They fall on him and take his life.

The scene of the Epilogue is the Red Square of Moscow. A rejoicing crowd sings the now famous "Slavsya" chorus acclaiming the new monarch. Among them we discover Antonida and Vanya, whose grief causes general astonishment until their names become known: it is then that the great Trio is sung. Amid general rejoicing the curtain falls for the last time.

III.

Heard apart from the context, the overture to " A Life for the Tsar " hardly conveys to us at this date the impression of being great music. Naturally, when it is considered in relation to the opera as a whole, it gains enormously in interest. It cannot be denied that it admirably fulfils the function of an operatic overture in being a key to the music that follows it. Thus, after a few introductory chords the oboe plaintively hints at Vanya's lament to be heard at length in the famous Trio in the Epilogue. Following this, there are suggestions both of the music that accompanies Sobinin's preparations for the pursuit of the Poles, and of the Mazurka rhythm that is associated with them. The orphan's song, sung by Vanya in the peasant's hut before the interrupted wedding festivities have begun—one of the best-liked melodies in the work—is then foreshadowed. We realize that it belongs definitely to the foster-child when, in the forest scene, the doomed Soussanin has a vision of his son riding hard to warn the Tsar, for it is by this charming melody that the youth's gallant effort is musically referred to.*

One does not expect to find a closely knit system of leading motives, such as are to be traced in the music-dramas of Wagner. Still, as Cheshikin points out in his volume "The Russian Opera," there is a distinct connection between certain notable moments in Glinka's score—a link constituted by the Slavsya theme, or hymn of glory to the Tsar, which is the culminating point of the opera. This theme is omitted from the overture, and gains in effect by being reserved for the climax.

Dealing with this link Cheshikin calls attention to the quartet in the third act,† in which is to be found, as antiphonal response from the orchestra to the chorus "God, love the Tsar," a phrase containing a significant quotation from the "Slavsya." Again, when the Poles call upon Soussanin to lead them to the young Tsar's abode, his reply is sung to a melody which contains the outlines of the "Slavsya" and suggests also, by means of a fragment, that the Imperial theme is associated with the peasant who, a little while before, has been blessing the bridal pair.

This is only one of Glinka's methods of making an opera national. He has other means. One of the passages sung in the first act, "Greeting, Mother Moscow," is in imitation of a folk-melody, and the first

---

* In an analysis of the opera, K. Chernof mentions the resemblance between this and the Mephistophelian serenade in Berlioz' "Damnation of Faust."

† Cheshikin means the second act.

words declaimed by Soussanin are to the tune that
Glinka heard from the lips of a cabman.   The super-
cilious remark that this was *la musique des cochers*
came well from an audience that "stumbled in Russian
and chattered in French."

What must have appeared equally plebeian in that
quarter — it made a profound impression on the
orchestra during rehearsal—is the accompaniment to
the peasants' song of welcome when the rowers are
bringing Sobinin to shore on his return from Moscow.
It is in imitation of the balalaika.   It is not, however,
merely in the material employed that Glinka's method of
infusing into his opera a patriotic or nationalistic spirit
consists, but also in the manner of using it.   In the introductory peasants' chorus there is a specimen of the
traditional method of performing Russian folk-song,
in which a precentorial function is delegated to the
principal singer.   Another example of this is to be
found in Tchaikovsky's well-known opera "Evgenie
Oniegin."

Again, in the delightful nuptial chorus of the third
act, described by V. V. Stassof as "one of the finest
musical gems of our time," a $\frac{5}{4}$ rhythm has been used
in imitation of the irregular metrical arrangement of
the Russian folk-song.

The use of themes having a modal character is a
further expedient.   Its significance is revealed when
comparison between the folk-music of Russia and the
ancient church-tunes is made.   Glinka was one of the
first to observe this connection, spending, as we know,
the last year of his life in thoroughly investigating it.

In his "Arabesques" Gogol concludes a picturesque recital of the many sources from which Russian folk-song may be obtained with the observation that Glinka was fortunate in having two distinct founts from which to draw his themes—Russia and Poland. In reality, however, the composer's use of Polish rhythms is quite unconvincing. "Some critics," says Mrs. Newmarch in "The Russian Opera," "have supposed that the composer really wished to give an impression of the Poles as a superficial people literally dancing and revelling through life, and possessed of no deeper feelings to be expressed in music . . . It seems more probable that, not being super-saturated with Polish as he was with Russian folk-music, he found it difficult to indicate the personality of the Pole in anything but conventional dance-rhythms. This passes well enough in the second act, where the scene is laid at a brilliant festival in the Polish capital, and the ballroom dances that follow constitute the ballet of the opera. But in the other parts of the work, as, for instance, when the Polish soldiers burst into Soussanin's cottage and order him to act as their guide, the strains of a stately Polonaise seem distinctly out of place; and again, when they have lost their way in the forest and their situation is extremely precarious, they express their alarm and suspicion in Mazurka rhythm."

Glinka in this respect is of course not much worse a sinner than Moussorgsky, whose Polish act in "Boris Godounof" is certainly—and mainly for the same reason—much below the standard of the rest.

IV.

It has been remarked that Glinka was unable in
" A Life for the Tsar " to shake off the influence of
Italy and the stereotyped cast of the Italian melodic
line.   It has also been observed that he did not succeed
in severing the bonds that tethered him to the un-
reality and insincerity of the opera of a preceding
generation.   If in some of his music we see plentiful
evidence of a desire to cultivate a Russian style, we are
obliged to confess at the same time that that growth
is threatened by a musical turn of phrase that may
well be compared to the convolvulus.   Such a melody,
for instance, as Antonida's Cavatina is as Russian in
the main as could be, but the flourishes that adorn it
are as Italian as what César Cui refers to as the inevitable top note at the end of the song.

When, however, the same critic speaks of the initial
solo allotted to Antonida as having been designed to
give the prima-donna a brilliant _entrée,_ he does not
make it clear that this was the specific intention of the
composer as is shown by his first sketch-plan of " A
Life for the Tsar." This should not be overlooked,
as it serves as valuable evidence of Glinka's rather
faint-hearted attitude towards the abuses that were so
much more resolutely faced some years later by
Dargomijsky and Moussorgsky. Glinka's work was,
as Gogol prophetically observed, a happy beginning.

There is a real need to dwell upon such points as
these when addressing readers of a generation remote

from that in which " A Life for the Tsar " was regarded
as a phenomenon by the operatic world. It is necessary that we should train our eyes to look at the work
in a proper perspective. Most of the masterpieces of
the Russian reformers have been heard in England at
a date so long after their composition and production
that the reforms embodied in them have no longer the
same appearance of novelty. When " A Life for the
Tsar " comes once again to be performed in England,
much of the music that lies in the pages of its score
will sound old-fashioned. But the nationalistic spirit
that pervades them has not evaporated, and the opera
might well be used by the student of Russia as a com-
plementary document. It will provide an insight into
the character and customs, as well as the history of
the Russian people, that is not to be derived from the
volumes designed for that purpose.

What " A Life for the Tsar " meant to the student
of its day may be gathered from the lines written by
Henri Mérimée, the brother of the librettist of " Car-
men." They were penned in 1840, four years after
the production of the opera, and are quoted in the
composer's autobiography.

" Glinka's ' Life for the Tsar ' is extraordinarily
original, the first work of art that has not borrowed
anything. . . . Poetically as well as musically, it is
a faithful account of all that Russia has suffered and
sung, in it are to be discovered her love and her hate,
her lamentations and her rejoicings, her gloomy nights
and her radiant dawns, it is at first a mournful plaint,
but this gives place to a hymn of redemption so proud

and so triumphant that the emotions of the obscurest peasant brought from his hut into the theatre could not fail to be stirred to their very depths. It is more than an opera, it is a national epic, it is the lyric drama re-endowed with a nobility long remote from it, a nobility that belonged to it in the times when it was not a mere frivolous amusement, but a solemn and patriotic ceremony. Although a foreigner, I have never witnessed a representation without experiencing a lively and sympathetic emotion."

The reverent attitude of this appreciative Frenchman is in part due to his thorough respect for the music. Such terms as "national epic" may seem a little extravagant to the present generation.

In reality they are quite fitting.

V.

In the spring of 1913 the Emperor Nicholas II. undertook a pilgrimage to the centres traversed by the first Romanof when called to the throne by election in February, 1613. Accompanied by his family, the Tsar proceeded first to the ancient town of Souzdal. In its monastery is the tomb of Prince Pojarsky who, three hundred years ago, placed himself at the head of a volunteer army recruited from Nijni-Novgorod, and defeated the Poles under Shotkevich. From thence the royal pilgrim travelled to Nijni-Novgorod, visiting there the tomb of Kuzma Minin " of the dry hand," butcher and magistrate, who in 1613 prevailed

upon his fellow-citizens to devote a third of their
worldly belongings to the patriotic purpose of equipping
and maintaining Pojarsky's warriors.

Following the course of the Volga, the party next
came to Kostroma, in whose monastery lived the founder
of the present Russian dynasty. The personal and
historical relics of Michael Romanof preserved in the
museum were reverently inspected. Here the Tsar
received a deputation of the "White Ploughers," the
appellation by which the progeny of the peasant
Soussanin are distinguished. An order was issued
exempting them from every kind of taxation. "The
population of those regions which produced Filaret
(the father of Michael Romanof) and Minin, Pojarsky
and Palitzyn, Hermogenes and a thousand stalwart
defenders of the Fatherland," says a chronicler of the
pilgrimage,* "have not degenerated. . . . To see these
people, to converse with them, to be within the sphere
of their spiritual influence, is tantamount to deriving
new spiritual forces, new energies and knowledge. . . ."

When, therefore, in listening to Glinka's "Life for
the Tsar" we hear Sobinin repeat the words of Prince
Pojarsky to his people, "My children, let us show our
valour!" when the chorus echoes his words, "Com-
rades! to horse," we ought to remember that it is
the Pojarsky near to whose tomb the Tsar began his
commemorative progress. When we hear the messenger announcing to the assembled Polish nobles that
the claims of their sovereign Ladislas have been

* S. N. Syromiatnikof, in *The Times* Russian Supplement,
June 16, 1913.

disregarded by the Russians, that the son of Filaret Romanof has been chosen by the Muscovites as Tsar, that the newly elected monarch is as yet ignorant of his promotion to royal rank, being at present secluded in his Kostroma abode, we should bear in mind that this Filaret is the father of the man to whose memory Nicholas II. rendered homage.

Lastly, to observe the resemblance of Soussanin's musical utterances to the " Slavsya " theme, without recalling the heroic peasant's relationship to the White Ploughers, so fittingly honoured by their Emperor, would be to accord to " A Life for the Tsar " only half the attention it merits.

It may thus be seen that Mérimée's language is not to be carelessly dismissed as hyperbole. And if we find ourselves wondering at Glinka's confession that the music sung by Soussanin in the forest made the composer's hair rise in horror by its successful evocation of appropriate emotions, let us not blame the father of Russian Opera for that we neglected his score until he had become the grandfather.

" RUSSLAN AND LUDMILLA."

VI.

If " A Life for the Tsar " is to be regarded as a national epic, Glinka's second opera " Russlan and Ludmilla " must be credited with a significance equally nationalistic, though in a different region. " A Life for the Tsar " is directly national, " Russlan and

Ludmilla " indirectly. The former work is in the nature of a historical document; the latter a poetical.

Russian folk-lore is not always entirely remote from history; in some instances the stirring episodes of an Empire's record have become the textual substance of traditional song. But the folk-lore material of " Russlan and Ludmilla " is altogether of a fantastic nature. The supernatural element is not merely a convenience by which a plot may be invested with a greater power; it is the main foundation of the plot.

Considered as the model after which many subsequent Russian operatic works have been fashioned, Glinka's second contribution to the theatre assumes an importance quite independent of that with which we credit it by virtue of its purely musical and dramatic qualities.

That the influence of " Russlan and Ludmilla " is responsible for such creations as have since been given to the world by Dargomijsky, Borodin, Rimsky-Korsakof, and Stravinsky, can easily be grasped by anyone conversant with the history of music in Russia prior to and since the time of Glinka. Such operas as Rimsky-Korsakof's " Kashchei," " Tsar Saltan," " The Snow-Maiden," " Sadko," and " Kitej," and Stravinsky's " Firebird " ballet, have all a foundation in a folk-lore in which the supernatural predominates. But there are other elements than this to support this opera's claim to the distinction of being a pioneer work. It is in " Russlan and Ludmilla " that Oriental colour is for the first time used in Russian music. Glinka perceived the advantage that would accrue to the art-nationalist who should think imperially, and his adoption of this principle has endowed Russian music with a source of melody that has since been heavily drawn upon. Opera is not the only region in which the benefit of Glinka's policy has been felt. Balakiref's piano fantasia "Islamey"—a veritable epic of the Orient—Borodin's "In the Steppes of Central Asia," and Rimsky-Korsakof's "Sheherazade" all owe their inspiration to "Russlan and Ludmilla." In each case a sensibility to eastern colour was inherent, but the impulse to express the Orient in music originated in Glinka's example.

When, in 1818, Pushkin read to the circle of which Glinka afterwards became a member the initial verses of his poem "Russlan and Ludmilla," he caused a sensation not altogether unlike that which greeted the manifestations of nationalism in "A Life for the Tsar." By the more reasonable it was characterized as a parody of Kirsha Danilof, whose collection of Russian folk-material was the pioneer effort of its kind. A reviewer of the period, evidently of the same feather as the objector to "cabmen's music," resented the introduction of "an unkempt peasant into a drawing-room."

What is of considerable value to the student either of the literature, the music, or of the social progress of Russia, is that neither the friends who welcomed the innovation nor its depreciators seem to have been aware that the poem is not in the true folk-style. Russian society, dominated by foreign influence, has ever been slow in discovering its own national characteristics. This has often been the subject of ironical comment on the part of literary men: Gogol never tired of exposing the anomaly, and in recent times we have had an example in music constituted by the Russian musical dilettante's readiness to accept the "elegant (but quite personal) pessimism" of Tchaikovsky as a genuine musical expression of race.

But Pushkin had at any rate made a beginning. The almost superstitious respect for alien art had been attacked, and the material for a truly national literature soon followed.

The Prologue of the poet's "Russlan and Ludmilla" introduces the reader to the famous and miraculous cat that, circling around a great oak-tree, spends day and night in stimulating a belief in the fairies. When he turns to the right he sings a song, when he goes leftwards a tale he tells.

It is at his feet, Pushkin tells us, that one must sit, if one would seek to know the ancient Russian legend, to hear about the "russalki," the terrible Kashchei, and Baba Yaga in her hut on fowls' legs. . . .

"I," says Pushkin, "am seated under the oak and hear the cat's stories; this is what he told me."

VII.

Following is the substance of the libretto compiled by the several hands, enumerated on another page. The first act takes us to the festivities which are being held by Prince Svyetozar of Kief, in honour of the suitors of his daughter, Ludmilla: the knight-errant Russlan, a warm-blooded Tatar Prince, Ratmir, and the faint-hearted Varangian, Farlaf. It is on the first that the young Princess smiles, and Svyetozar ordains that the marriage be forthwith celebrated. But the mortals have not reckoned with the plans of the evil spirits. Hardly is the invocation to Lel, the god of Love, finished, than a thunder-clap is heard and darkness descends upon the scene. When the light returns it is seen that the Princess is missing. Svyetozar makes it known that he will bestow his daughter on the one who discovers her whereabouts and brings her safely home. The three suitors at once take up the challenge and set out on their search.

The second act has three scenes, the first being the cave of Finn, a sorcerer and Russlan's good genius. To him Finn imparts the knowledge that Ludmilla has been carried off by Chernomor, the wonder-working dwarf who has become enamoured of the Princess. Finn instructs the young knight in the method by which he may hope to regain his betrothed, warns him against the machinations of Naina, who after repeated refusals to listen to Finn's avowal of love has relented too late, indicates the path to be taken and wishes him God-speed.

In the second scene we overtake Farlaf, who has already begun to despair. Meeting Naina, he is advised by her to abandon his search and to reap his advantage by stealing the lost lady from him who

5

finds her. She promises to provide against the
opposition of both Russlan and Ratmir.

· A further change of scene enables us to follow the
fortunes of the hero. Russlan has arrived at a deserted
battle-field shrouded in mist and strewn with the
relics of a remote combat. Among them he finds a
spear and a shield. Presently through the mist, which
has become thinner, Russlan perceives the severed
head of a giant who is the brother of the fearful
Chernomor. In self-protection the Head blows from
its cavernous mouth a storm, but is overcome by
Russlan's spear-thrust. Under the Head our knight
finds the magic sword with which he is destined to
rescue Ludmilla.

The third act takes place in the enchanted palace
of Naina, whose acquaintance has already been made.
There is a chorus of beautiful Persian maidens, followed by an entreaty addressed by Gorislava to the
errant Ratmir, who has deserted her for another.
Her appeal is answered in person by the young Oriental,
but her victory is only momentary, for Ratmir's
attention is soon absorbed by the other maidens who
surround and fascinate him. A similar fate threatens
to overtake Russlan, who meanwhile has entered.
From it he is saved by the timely appearance of Finn,
whose warning has been disregarded. Under Finn's
magic power Naina's castle collapses. Gorislava and
Ratmir are re-united, and Russlan is free to continue
his search for Ludmilla.

In the fourth act he finds her a captive in the enchanted domain of Chernomor. Overcome by weari-

ness, she is sleeping. Presently the ogre appears in the midst of his minions and, seating himself beside Ludmilla, issues a command that the festivities arranged for her entertainment shall be continued. It is then that Russlan appears. Chernomor hastily plunges Ludmilla into a trance, and goes forth to meet the intruder.

Russlan, aided by the magic sword, is victorious, but his triumph is tempered by his failure to awaken Ludmilla. Gorislava and Ratmir now join him, and on their advice he begins the journey back to Kief.

The opening of the first scene of the fifth and last act quickly recalls that Russlan's second rival has yet to be dealt with. Ludmilla has been filched from her rescuer by Farlaf.

Chernomor's spell, which has not yet been broken, now stands the lovers in good stead, for Farlaf, who in the final scene brings back Ludmilla to her home at Kief, has to confess himself powerless to penetrate her slumber. Deliverance comes with the arrival of Russlan, bearing a magic ring, the gift of Finn. With this he breaks the spell, and the opera concludes with a general rejoicing.

VIII.

The music of "Russlan and Ludmilla" shows an advance, in technical power as in style, altogether out of proportion to the few years that separate it from the composer's first work. While Glinka had not yet divested himself of the formalism of which he was at

once the heir and the victim, he nevertheless shows
that he had emancipated himself to a quite considerable extent from the stylistic absurdities of traditional
opera. Seeing that his reforms fell altogether short
of those mooted by Dargomijsky, one is justified in
supposing that had Glinka followed the composer of
" The Stone Guest " instead of preceding him, he might
have achieved something even greater than " Boris
Godounof."

In " Russlan and Ludmilla " we still find that
solicitousness in regard to the "rights " of the *prima-
donna;* the high C to which Cui calls our attention in
" A Life for the Tsar " is again to be seen and, one may
be sure, to be heard in the later work. There are
pages altogether lacking in refinement; but these are
far outnumbered by the many evidences of lofty genius
which are so easily discoverable in the score.

One very noticeable quality in the music of " Russlan
and Ludmilla " is apparently due to the influence of
Dehn. To the German's teaching we may surely
attribute both the presence of certain classical forms
and the attempt to employ contrapuntal devices.
That counterpoint of which Glinka professed at one
time to have such a dread, considering it the enemy
of inspiration, now appears as its ally. The composer
had discovered that counterpoint, though a bad master,
is an excellent servant.

The appearance of the tonal scale as a leading
motive in " Russlan and Ludmilla " has misled more
than one commentator. Any endeavour to trace its
connection with the fully developed system that has

proved so disastrous an obsession in the composers of *fin-de-siècle* France is bound to fail.

The use of a characteristic scale passage as a pictorial device—it is generally associated with terror—appears to have begun in Russia, and seems to have remained there. Among those who, beside Glinka, have drawn upon it may be mentioned Dargomijsky, Moussorgsky, Tchaikovsky, Rimsky-Korsakof, and Rakhmaninof. The employment of the complete harmonic system, based on the tonal scale, by such as Rebikof and Debussy is not traceable to the influence that in other directions has most certainly been derived by these composers from the earlier Russian masters.

Glinka's introduction of the Oriental element into " Russlan and Ludmilla " cannot perhaps be considered as a great stroke of genius. But his manner of effecting it is nothing less than that. The significance of the presence of Eastern melody is not lessened by the circumstance that more than one of these tunes was handed complete to the composer by friends and acquaintances who had enjoyed excellent opportunities of hearing them in a proper environment. Glinka might easily have displayed the *naïveté* betrayed by several Western composers in allocating and harmonizing these melodies. But it is precisely in this particular that he scores a triumph. The Eastern music, and no less, be it said, the postillion's song, brought from Imatra, are placed and harmonized with such a complete appropriateness as to give an impression that they are an integral part of the music that emerged from the composer's store of original melody.

It is this impression of rightness and inevitability that has caused the Oriental idea in music to become so popular among Russian composers. Such an idea was bound to be exploited sooner or later by men who, from their childhood, had only to look round them to see how closely Oriental colour and design is intermingled in the poetic, pictorial, and decorative arts with the purely Slavonic. But if the first attempt had been at all lacking in spontaneity, the result must have been very different. Orientalism would have been looked upon as a particular feature in a single work, and not, as it now is, as a predominant characteristic of the Russian School as a whole.

IX.

The overture of " Russlan and Ludmilla " is in curious contrast to that of " A Life for the Tsar." It contains so small an amount of the musical material contained in the subsequent pages as to be very little representative of it. Another point of difference is that instead of avoiding a full statement of the opera's final apotheosis this overture begins with one. Following upon this introduction comes the penultimate chorus of thanksgiving which in the last scene succeeds Ludmilla's awakening. The overture consists of very little beyond the simultaneous development of these two themes—Chernomor's tonal scale joining the second of them as a contrapuntal accompaniment of the passage that leads into the Coda.

The overture is followed by an introduction in which the Bayan (or Skald) takes a leading part. The music of this section is suitable in every respect. The Bayan's utterances are introduced by means of passages suggestive of the gusli on which he accompanies himself. The music generally has an appropriate air of the archaic and the heroic. The function of the Bayan is that of establishing Pushkin's poem as the basis of the action. This he does in the poet's own words. Once that task is fulfilled, and having supplied the material for a fine chorus in $\frac{6}{4}$ measure, he vanishes from the scene, and the opera can really be said only to begin with Ludmilla's Cavatina—and a very inauspicious beginning it is ! Ere the eight bars of introduction are over, it is abundantly clear that in composing these pages the singer, and not the music, was uppermost in Glinka's thoughts. It should be added that this was no ordinary singer.

The section of the score immediately following contains some of the most remarkable moments in the opera. The chorus to Lel, the god of Love (a personage who makes an appearance in Rimsky-Korsakof's symbolical opera " The Snow-Maiden "), is superior to that in similar rhythm ($\frac{5}{4}$) in " A Life for the Tsar." Beginning in unison the voices break out into a splendid invocation to the traditional words, " Lido, Lado ! Lel !" after which the refrain is resumed by the sopranos and altos in sixths. A further unison passage is interrupted by the thunder-clap preceding the darkness under cover of which Ludmilla is abducted by Chernomor's agents. It is then that Glinka begins to

pay homage to Dehn.   The panic that follows Chernomor's coup is musically portrayed by means of a vocal
canon, the orchestra remaining on a prolonged tonic
pedal, which lasts until the light returns.

The music introducing the second act is of an
appropriate kind.   Foreshadowing the theme to be
used for the Narration of the severed Head, it deals,
as may be gathered, with the most conspicuous figure
in the act; this procedure resembles that of the overture,
since its principal subject-matter is not reached until
the last number of the act it introduces.   The Ballad
of Finn that immediately succeeds the Prelude is
among the choicest music in the opera.   For this
refrain (the postillion's song) Glinka has found a
harmonic scheme that fits both the melody and its
text as though part of a triple creation.   The changes
of key and mode which are designed to emphasize the
variety of guises in which the sorcerer has attempted
the captivation of Naina form an admirable example
of the Russo-Oriental method of variation, of which
there is a further specimen in the Persian chorus.

The sturdy theme of Russlan's search for weapons
on the deserted battle-field is one of several that lead
one to suppose Glinka to have diligently studied the
classics during his sojourn in Berlin.   It might well
have been the subject of an old-time fugue.   The
storm that ensues on his discovery of the Head is
devoid of any novelty or ingenuity; it is chromatic and
conventional.

The prelude to the third act again suggests the
student.   It was apparently not intended to have any

connection with its dramatic context, and is admirably described by M. Calvocoressi as wearing the appearance of a page torn from Bach's "Forty-eight." Overleaf is material of a very different order. The famous Persian chorus is one of the most alluring operatic numbers in Russian musical literature, and its influence has been exceedingly wide. It was probably a desire to emulate his forerunner that drove Moussorgsky to introduce the Persian dances into his "Khovansh-china." This explanation is rather more satisfactory than the somewhat flimsy one hitherto advanced. Rimsky-Korsakof frankly avows the indebtedness of " Antar " to this purely decorative number in " Russlan and Ludmilla."

In the Cavatina of this act Glinka reverts once more to the classical style. Writing, many years after the production of the opera, to a friend, he acquaints him of the discovery in Handel's " Samson " of an aria resembling this commonplace melody. By a curious coincidence the aria in which Ratmir responds to the foregoing Cavatina has been described by M. Bellaigue as the work of " an Oriental Handel." The remainder of the music of this act falls rather below the level of the first portion, the dances intended to bring about Ratmir's downfall possessing little of the seductiveness attributed to them by the composer.

In the next *entr'acte* Glinka once more avoids principal themes, using that accompanying Chernomor's defeat and death and ignoring the bearded ogre's. March, also the " russalka " music and the chorus of Harmonious Flowers, in which the composer uses his wood-wind with a mastery equal to that of Tchai-kovsky. A moment later the leading violin is honoured in the manner associated with Rimsky-Korsakof.

X.

Chernomor's March is a piece of descriptive music that has many prototypes among the works of Glinka's successors. It is written on Pushkin's programme, and is a splendid portrait of the hoary - bearded monster.

Then come the Oriental dances that have been popularized of late years by inclusion in the arrange-ment known as " Cleopatra," a ballet in which the music of a number of Russian composers has been collected. The first is Turkish; the second is an Arab dance, the most distinguished of the three; and the third the famous Caucasian Lezginka, the theme of which was given to Glinka by Aivazovsky. The last-named dance is full of original harmonies which seem extraordinarily bold even to the modern musician. It soon achieved a world-wide renown, and was played in a transcription by Liszt at Petrograd in the year following the production of the opera.

Following this *divertissement* comes the aerial con-flict between tyrant and rescuer, in which the descend-ing tonal scale personifies the former. The act con-cludes with a grave Marcia Allegro risoluto, which is compared by a commentator with Beethoven's " Vivace alla Marcia," op. 101.

The last *entr'acte*, built on the themes associated with Ludmilla's slumber, is in A minor, the final chord having a sharpened third. The abrupt transition to D flat major seems to have been adopted in order to produce in the music the effect of the complete change of scene. One must add, however, that Ratmir's Romance, the first number of the final act, is admirably suited by this tonality. The concluding act contains other music qualified to rank with the foregoing, to which Serof accorded the distinction of being one of Glinka's finest lyrical inspirations. The melody sung by Finn when handing the magic ring to Ratmir is especially beautiful. It has a superficial resemblance to the theme of the duet between Vanya and Soussanin in the third act of Glinka's other opera. A fragment is transformed with considerable ingenuity into the music already referred to as portraying Ludmilla's slumber. This metamorphosis is a piece of subtlety comparable with that displayed in the use of the " Slavsya " motive in " A Life for the Tsar." A slightly different version of the complete theme is heard at the moment of Ludmilla's awakening, when the rescued maiden repeats it in a dreamy voice. It may be mentioned that the singer entrusted with this rôle has to be fully awake when, a few bars later, she closes her solo with a high C and a florid scale passage ! The rest of the act is familiar as the music of the overture, now used for the purpose of glorifying the benevolent deities.

Thus ends the opera that Stassof considers worthy to take a prominent place not merely among the works of Glinka, but among those of the whole musical world.

PART III

SYMPHONIC AND VOCAL WORKS

I.

As a composer of symphonic music, Glinka holds a place in the annals of Russian musical history no less honourable than that accorded him by common consent in virtue of his operatic achievements.

The first of those orchestral fantasies by means of which, as has been mentioned, Glinka hoped to appeal to the greater or "general" public without in any way lowering the standard of his ideals, was the Caprice on the theme of the "Jota Aragonesa," composed at Madrid in 1845.

In it Glinka employed what has now become the conventional paraphernalia of Spanish music. The convention is the legacy of Glinka, its discovery is his. When listening to the Spanish overture, composed many years later by Balakiref, one would do well to remember that its very existence is due to the earlier composer, who bequeathed to the leader of the "New Russian School" not only the manner, but the matter —namely, the theme used by Balakiref. Rimsky-Korsakof, in his Spanish Caprice, which it need hardly be said also owes its inspiration to this source, has chosen the same path to that honourable popularity which was Glinka's avowed goal.

Each composer has elected to heighten the interest of his score by means of the introduction of instrumental responsibility. The various instrumentalists are given work to do which increases their own interest as well as, through their performance of it, the public's. Rimsky-Korsakof, being a progressive musician, developed this responsibility of Glinka's instrumentalist into the virtuosity of his own. This may be clearly observed by reference both to the Spanish Caprice and " Sheherazade."

Glinka's second Spanish work for orchestra was the " Souvenir of a Summer Night in Madrid," composed in 1849. This does not, like the earlier piece, concern itself with one main theme, but is a monument to the industrious research undertaken by the composer during the first period of his visit to Spain. It contains a Jota which has little in common with that of the Caprice, a Punto Moruno, and two contrasted Seguidillas Manchegas.

The " Kamarinskaya " has done for orchestral music in Russia what " A Life for the Tsar " has achieved for Opera. " With ' Kamarinskaya,' " says Rimsky-Korsakof in his Memoirs, " Glinka bequeathed to posterity the symphonic treatment of the Russian folk-tune." " Without intending to compose anything beyond a simple humorous trifle," wrote Tchaikovsky in his diary, " he has left us a little masterpiece every bar of which is the outcome of enormous creative power. Half a century has passed since then, and many Russian symphonic works have been composed. . . . The germ of all this lies in ' Kamarinskaya,' as the oak-tree lies in the acorn. For long years to come Russian composers will drink at this source. . . ."

But the wedding song and dance that serve as thematic material in this little masterpiece are handled with a dexterity that has never yet been surpassed by any of those who have striven to emulate the discoverer of Russian musical nationalism.

II.

The music to Kukolnik's "Prince Kholmsky," a drama dealing with the political affairs of Pskof and Livonia in the fifteenth century, bears further testimony to the composer's genius. Its style, as a whole, is a compromise between the classical and the romantic. At times, as in the case of the second subject ($\frac{6}{8}$) treated in the overture, it possesses a Slavonic flavour. The Hebrew song in which the Jewess Rachael describes "the past glories of her race," is not without the grandeur required of the music by its text, though its Hebraic character is not at all marked. The song of the Nurse Illinichna, "Blows the Tempest through the Gate," has something of the spirit of the Russian folk-dance.

The music of the prelude to the third act is the most charming but perhaps the least appropriate. Considering that it is supposed to introduce the avowal of Prince Kholmsky's love for the Livonian Baroness Adelheid, a confession that carries with it the promise to sever his allegiance to the Russian Tsar, this very fascinating ball-room refrain seems, to say the least of it, hardly an adequate preparation for so dramatic a moment. This, together with the next symphonic number, fails to reach the level attained by the music preceding the fifth act, so far, that is, as concerns dramatic power. One would prefer indeed to judge the whole as music without reference to its programme. Thus considered, one is more inclined to agree with Serof who, after comparing " Prince Kholmsky " with " Egmont," prophesies that at some future time the world will accord to Glinka the place among European composers to which his genius fully entitles him.

III.

In appraising the merits of Glinka's vocal music one does not feel justified in crediting him with having written ahead of his own generation. As a vocal writer he followed the line of least resistance, giving a broad Cantilena to the voice and a simply harmonized accompaniment to the piano. The composer was assisted in his design of the melody by his own experience as a singer, and by the knowledge acquired during the lessons from Belloli. With a few exceptions his songs cannot be said to break new ground. They were composed without any other than the melodic purpose in view, and if Glinka's intention was that they, like his orchestral fantasies, should appeal to the larger public of his day, he may be considered to have fully realized such a hope; his songs became very popular, and he had no difficulty in disposing of them, in some instances at a very fair price.

They are mostly admirable specimens considered in relation to contemporary vocal art. Such examples as " The Lark " and " Doubt " stand out, of course, as bearing evidence of inspiration; but they have not the claim to our attention as have such as the wonderfully dramatic setting of Joukovsky's "Midnight Review" and "The Northern Star," in which Glinka introduces a reminiscence of the Wedding Song of "Kamarinskaya." Generally speaking, Glinka's songs proclaim the artist rather than the pioneer.

*   *   *   *   *

It does not seem improbable that, but for his travels and the resultant musical nostalgia, his operas, if in such circumstances he had composed for the theatre, would have had no greater purpose than his songs.

But the call of Russia, heard in climes so utterly remote from the steppes, aroused in the "father of Russian Opera" the instinct to create that which the art of his country most needed. " A Life for the Tsar " inaugurated a tradition that appears to have lapsed with the decline of the primitive nationalist propaganda. There seems a likelihood, however, that composers of the contemporary schools may feel called upon to revive that tradition. Fortunately Russia is to-day so rich in musical genius that she need fear no difficulty in finding the man when the hour shall arrive.

As for the tradition of "Russlan and Ludmilla," this has never lapsed. There are few among the Slavonic School who could prove themselves to have remained without the sphere of its influence. Were Russia to become "westernized" until every semblance of nationality had been blotted out from the character of its people, the influence of that work would cease from exerting itself upon Russian Music. But not until then.

LIST OF GLINKA'S PRINCIPAL WORKS

OPERAS.

A Life for the Tsar. (1836.)
Russlan and Ludmilla. (1842.)

When twenty years of age Glinka made some sketches for an opera based on Sir Walter Scott's " Rokeby." These are preserved in the Petrograd Imperial Public Library.

ORCHESTRA.

A Summer Night in Madrid. (1848.)
Jota Aragonesa. (1848.)
Kamarinskaya. (1848.)
Valse-Fantasia. (1839. Revised 1856.)
Polonaise for the Coronation of Alexander II. (1855.)
Incidental music for Kukolnik's drama " Prince Kholmsky.
     (1840.)

CHAMBER MUSIC.

" Pathetic " Trio, for piano, clarinet and bassoon. (1827
String quartet. (1836.)
Sextet, for piano and strings. (1834.)

PIANO.

About 20 pieces, comprising Polkas, Mazurkas, Nocturnes and Variations, among which may be mentioned:

      Scottish [sic] Theme with variations.*
      Variations on Alabief's " Nightingale."
      Variations on a theme of Mozart.
      Capriccio on Little-Russian themes.

* The tune is a version of "The Last Rose of Summer," the character of which is destroyed by the appearance of the subdominant.

CHORAL MUSIC.

Cantata in memory of Alexander I., for Solo, Chorus and
   Orchestra.   (1826.)

Cantatas for the Catherine Institute (1841) and the Smolensk
   Convent (1856); for women's Chorus, Solo and Orchestra.

Cantata for Tenor, Chorus and Orchestra.   (Posthumous.)

Polish Hymn, for Chorus and Orchestra.   (1837.)

Of the 70 songs the following are the best known:

> The Midnight Review.
> I am here, Inezilia.
> Doubt.
> I think of that Enchanting Moment.
> The Northern Star.
> To Molly.
> The Lark.
> Gretchen's Song.

INDEX

PRINTED BY BILLING AND SONS, LTD., GUILDFORD, ENGLAND.

CPSIA information can be obtained
at www.ICGtesting.com
Printed in the USA
BVHW051257040219
539409BV00029B/2387/P